Blahník by Boman

Blahník by Boman

Shoes, Photographs, Conversation

CHRONICLE BOOKS

SAN FRANCISCO

introduction by Paloma Picasso

Early friendships are like a triptych mirror in which you can discover yourself. When Manolo, Eric and I first met, none of us had yet found the best channel to reveal our vision. We shared the same passion for going to the movies, old and new, and for rummaging through flea markets in search of objects or clothes that were more in tune with our tastes than what was on offer at the time. Choosing is always the first step to creating your own style. Stating our differences and agreements with great assertion and great laughs, having a definitive opinion on what our new standards should be, was at the centre of our discussions, and we came to know each other to the core. The fact is that what we are doing today is just a logical extension of what we determined back then.

I met Manolo in Paris when I was still at school. He already stood out as a sophisticated, fascinating young man with a mind like a wayward comet, full of fantasy and fun. I was sad to see him move to London, but he soon got to know Eric and arranged for the two of us to meet in Paris, where Eric had come to work. We hit it off immediately. He was not yet a photographer but an illustrator with a style of his own: very clean, to-the-point designs with a highly imaginative and poetic aspect. Being Scandinavian, a man from the North, he is in love with light and colour and how they interplay with shapes and volumes. Structure and composition, paired with a sense of play, are paramount in his work. It was only logical that Eric should turn to photography, where his insightful sensibility could be displayed. His images, which interact to enhance one another, are polished, and yet exude sensuality and emotions: a reflection of a refined and eclectic taste, a wealth of ideas, and a wicked sense of humour. Eric has a keen eye, as all artists should, for spotting and pairing the most unlikely elements, for finding the impossible balance – and that, surely, is what it's all about.

Manolo's exuberant conversation shoots in all directions. He may use four different languages in one sentence, but only to make sure that his ideas are properly communicated; and he works on his designs in the same way, with an abundance of references, razor-sharp engineering dexterity, manic attention to detail, and a personal aesthetic that can attain the sublime. Women go crazy for his shoes because when they step into their high heels they feel they are being elevated to semi-goddess status. If all the world is a stage, then you know your Manolos are your best prop.

Manolo works on his collections as though he were creating an encyclopedia of moods and desires.

He often appears to be making portraits of themes: "intensely baroque vegetal metamorphosis", "extravagantly exotic jungle fever feast", "sadistic tool of perverse bourgeoise", "romantic, demure, almost bashful cream puff", "pure understated minimalism of the strictest order", and so on. But then many of his creations also seem to embody characters in a play or a movie, giving multifaceted layers to their personalities. Nobody understands the theatricalization of glamour centred on the foot better than Manolo, who presents it as the pedestal we rest upon.

Eric has been able to give Manolo's creations the perfect settings in which to bloom before our eyes. He knows when to underline Manolo's hidden messages and when to challenge them by making a deliciously delirious and equally masterful counterpoint. It is very fitting that Eric and Manolo should have this conversation in visual terms – after all, those are the terms they mostly live their lives by. There is nothing contrived about it; it's the most natural way for them to express their friendship. Through this book you get a chance to peep at their real relationship and inner thoughts. Between them, they have invented a wonderful new genre of artistic dialogue.

[1/2] EB: Good morning! The soft and gentle colours of the early light. I don't see them very often. MB: The mist of Cantabria on an exhausting detour between Le Petit Trianon and Schönbrunn. [3] While filming "Barry Lyndon", Marisa Berenson pays a visit to Norma Shearer on the set of "Marie-Antoinette". Slightly misinterpreting the teachings of Rousseau, the Queen has ordered all the wigs for Le Hameau to be built over armatures of chicken wire. She thought it would contribute to the rusticity! I could see Kate Moss as Lady Lyndon today. And yet, the more I look at this, the more I believe it's the bedside chest of Proust's Princesse de Guermantes. [4/5] The most Gustavian spot in your house is in the cellar, with only a crack of daylight. It's a miracle we got this. You know, I really think the coral is my favourite of all! For me, it is "Il Gattopardo" – my favourite movie. The dewy beauty of Claudia Cardinale. How gloriously radiant when she dances with the Prince of Salina! Lily-of-the-valley tucked in her dress and hair. And how sexy when she bites her lower lip! [6/7] I imagined what might go on at floor level in an Ingres portrait. He didn't show us that very often. Or it could be a winter's afternoon in a parlour in Saint Petersburg, when only for a few hours the white, snow-reflected light filters into the room.... The copper lace bottine was never made – the sample so expensive it would have made it prohibitive. Well, at least we have this! [8/9] A boy offering the shoe to the world. The Fragonard mule looks like it's part of Peter [Schlesinger]'s bronze. The tasselled one is all about Eugenia de Montijo, who became Empress Eugénie, the royal shopaholic. The most fashionable empress ever! Did you know her obsession with detail encouraged hundreds of trades, like the makers of passementerie?

[10/11] **La Commedia dell'Arte!** Or Punch and Judy. Your harlequin has such a Leyendecker face, he must be from the 1920s. [12/13] It's hard to find really dark single lilacs these days; everybody grows double everything. But the most common lilac, so pale it's almost grey, has the best fragrance. **Le Paon Cacatoese! The screaming peacock! Where is the shoe? It's very small.** That's because these "petites mains" made a very large tail for it. [14/15] **The stripes of stripes: we cannot escape them.** College blazers are the best-looking. Maddeningly I outgrew one, of the most sublime colour combination – inch navy, half-inch sky blue and eighth-inch saffron yellow. Still thinking about it! [16/17] **La Belle Otero. She was from Barcelona – one of "Les Grandes Horizontales". What are those pieces of haberdashery? They could have been picked from one of her dresses, you know.** At my grandparents' house, I couldn't play with other children, because they lived on a farm and had muddy shoes, so I spent my days in the attic, snooping through old boxes. I found this Côte d'Or chocolate box, its label saying "White Lace" in my granny's hand, and in it was this ornament, saved from a dress from the late 1800s. It's handmade, and the flowers have little bits of raw cotton to plump them and make them seem more three-dimensional. It has stayed with me. **Piles of books on every surface – they are my life!** [18/19] Jamming, as in making jam, not jazz. I offer these redcurrants for comparison with my fake ones in plate 72, asking for trouble. **Schiaparelli strawberries!** Do you remember our plan to rescue the Schiaparelli boutique on the Place Vendôme? With Paloma – and Elsa's granddaughters, the Berenson girls – we were going to pool our combined talents. It seemed like a perfect idea. It never happened.

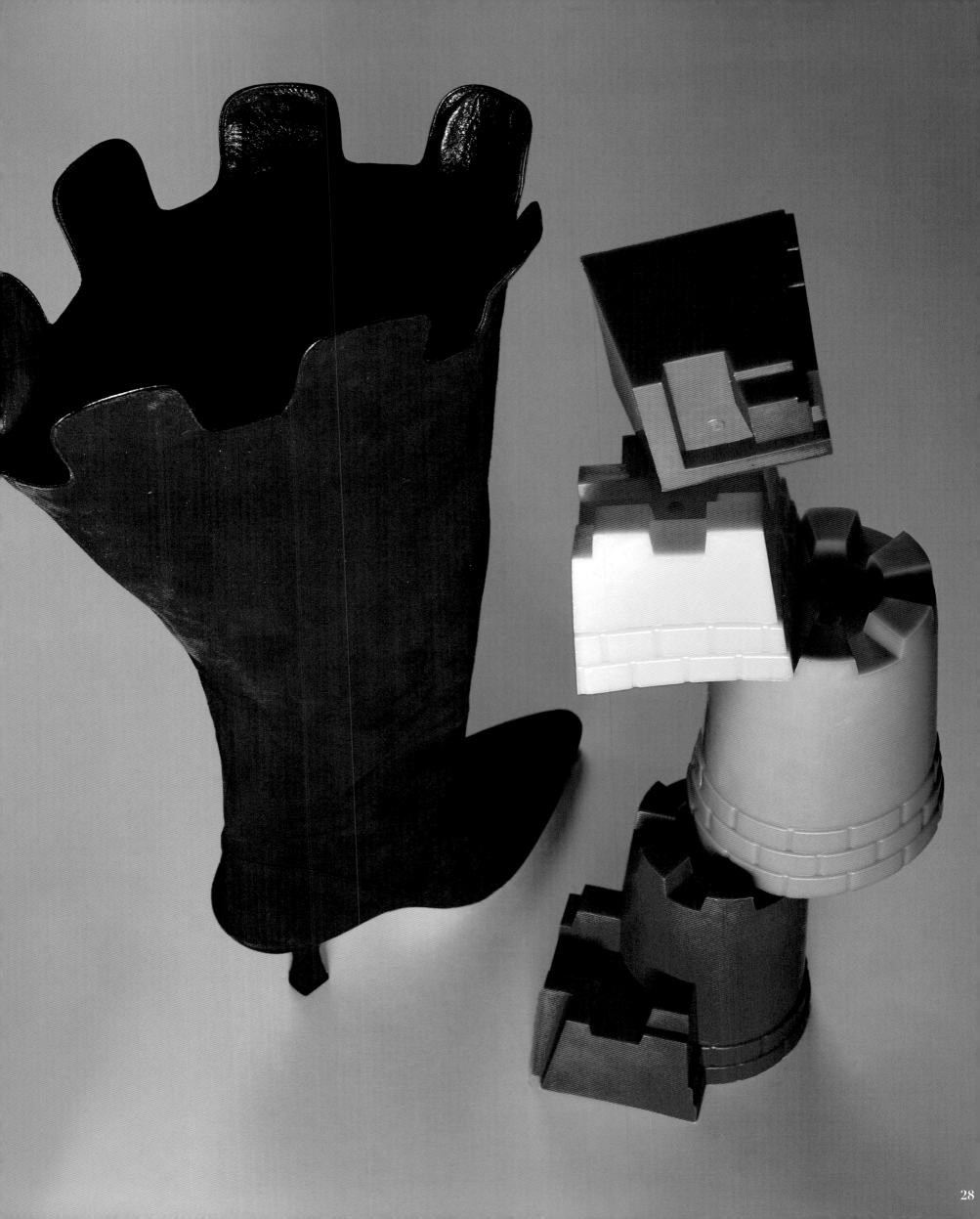

[20/21] Kay Kendall, with her ravishing Sargent profile, in Portofino, privately, on holiday, you understand … while a yet untamed young force-of-nature named Sophia Loren was running down the cobbled streets – clack-clopp! clack-clopp! – selling fish, shouting "Pesce, pesce" to Vittorio De Sica in "Pane, Amore e …". Or the eccentric American-in-Paris painter and celebrity gate-crasher Shirley Goldfarb, a very different kettle of fish. You knew her. I never did very well – only enough to buy her coffee at the Café de Flore. She was fun! Shirley wore shoes like these and had spiky lashes painted around her eyes with shiny eyeliner, like a Picasso plate from Vallauris. She was convinced all the waiters lusted after her. [22/23] We're now 225 feet under the surface of the Atlantic, off Nantucket, in the first-class salon of the "Andrea Doria", to pay homage to another collaboration of two friends: Gio Ponti and Piero Fornasetti. You and I didn't know each other in 1956, but we both remember where we were on July 26, when news of the collision with the M/S "Stockholm" reached Europe. **My papa had been playing tennis, and while showering he heard the news on our little Phillips transistor radio, pale lemon yellow, the most beautiful shape. I still have it.** Since it was the middle of summer, we were in the country in Sweden, where the news was taken very badly. We sat around the enormous Grundig all day. Only years later did I realize the full extent of the tragedy. In addition to fifty-two lives, the unequalled culmination of two of the greatest design talents of the time was lost – the jewel in Italy's transatlantic crown. The "Andrea Doria" was a daughter of Genoa, where the medieval buildings are built of black and white stone in horizontal stripes, and she was named for its greatest son. [24/25] **Vienna in the days of the Wiener**

Werkstätte. This is my Hoffman shoe. But the chair is Otto Wagner's Post Office Savings Bank model, here with a different back design. Like the ones Bavarian derrières perch upon when the ladies try on my shoes in Marion Heinrich's shop in Munich. The Klimt-like portrait of a dancer by Studio Ari is such a modern image. Joan Buck gave me the dice cufflinks thirty years ago. They were meant for a woman. Should I read anything into that? [26/27] This high heel-less shoe is a feat of engineering! But is it pretty? The citrus press from your kitchen seems to think so – it's smiling! You know, I re-invigorated the concept of the double heel. Don't forget the Japanese geta! It looks like a little creature. Can you walk on it? Of course you can! Well, not too far.... [28/29] Crenellation, castration and castanets! The sandcastle moulds are designed to take any creativity out of budding beach architects.... I feel superstitiously protective of this Japanese clog. It was the first thing I had published. Molly Parkin did it. A double page! That's typical – she gave me my first break, too. I made the clog with my hands. I'm so glad you can see the iridescence of the patent leather. [30/31] Linenfold panelling would have been good here. Tina Chow's bedroom had it, in pickled oak, but I hear the new people ripped it out. Isn't it ironic, by the way, that women go crazy for your high heels, but you love flat shoes just as much? Men think heels look sexier, but women know they feel sexier in them. The whole idea that men are more interested in sex is clearly dated.... You know, the blue picture is one of those things – I totally love it, but I don't have a clue what it is. Think of it as an underwater scene from an aquarium. Lord, it sounds like I'm suffering from some kind of submersion phobia. Do you think I should seek professional help?

MANOLO BLAHNIK

[32/33] The eighteenth century with a touch of the 1970s. Empress Josephine is visiting Lowestoft, making sure they send a set of china to the Hôtel Beauharnais at once! If you're Empress and your husband has renamed the months already, time travel is a concept you can deal with. [34/35] The translucence of Murano with the intellect of Dacia Maraini – a visual interpretation of crystalline poetry … faintly dusted with gold. I wasn't in her world, but had Mrs Vreeland firmly in my conscience. Her love of opulence! This is important: a "Vogue" from her reign. Is that Benedetta Barzini on the cover? With pencil strokes around her eyes, feathered like the pearls, and that "Swan Lake" head-dress? I'll find out. Remember when Paloma took us both to meet Mrs Vreeland at her office? Paloma's being by far the best name for securing an appointment! Mrs Vreeland told me to concentrate on shoes. And me to show my fabric designs to the man in the fur coat at Clarence House. [36/37] Spoiled little rich French boys, in shorts and knee-socks and navy sweaters buttoned on the shoulder, take their very fine sailboats to the basin in Le Jardin de Luxembourg. Like French Freddie Bartholomews – or you! "True Love" was the name of the boat in "The Philadelphia Story". Did you know I did my windows with lots of the exact same toy ones? I wondered what so many of them were doing in your attic. You have them in every colour! I'm so jealous. Lighthouses on the beach, not far in spirit…. [38/39] Les fruits de mer, selon arrivage … and an Arcimboldo foot. [40/41] Miss Sedgwick, meet Li'l Kim! Li'l Kim, meet Edie Sedgwick! A helium high at the first Warhol Factory. A terrible accident in the driveway of the very nice woman who lent me the car. She'd never heard of you! Where's the body? This is a book of still lifes.

[42/43] Our pets! Since your dogs live with your mamaita, I had to photograph your pet alligator. **That leaves your Alice as the only living creature in the book.** [44/45] **I adore the patchwork shoe! Nobody else likes it. It's not at all like seventies patchwork. I love that you can really see all the different textures.** That's why the French call a magnifying glass a "compte-fil" – for counting the threads. **But the teddy bears are too cutesy. [To the reader: cute is a swearword.]** They're your teddy bears from your childhood, and you do have them in this basket at the foot of your bed. [46/47] **A terracotta shoe!** Among the pots of Tage Zickerman. He potted in my grandparents' barn and taught me how to plant: dig a hole, fill it with water, put the plant in it, then press down the soil all around. It made a huge impression on me. He was ninety, I was five. **Opposite are oviform curves.** Peter brought home these wild turkey eggs. I said, "Wait a minute! Picture first, omelette later." [48/49] "The Leopard and the Giraffe" – a new La Fontaine fable! [50] An African village street at sunset. In their mud and straw huts, the women are preparing the evening meal. Grains, roots and Coca-Cola. Through the acrid smoke of dung fires, you hear the distant sound of elephants trumpeting. Africa has been my greatest source of inspiration! Again and again, I come back to it. [51/52] On the verandah of a Kenyan farm with Mr Sandow, the first bodybuilder pinup. He was obviously very keen on wild-cat furs – the caveman look – and fashioned a variety of loincloths from ocelot. My first love was leopard! But isn't Lee Krasner on the wrong safari? You cannot claim an entire continent for yourself. The Abstract Expressionists had a thing about Africa too, you know.

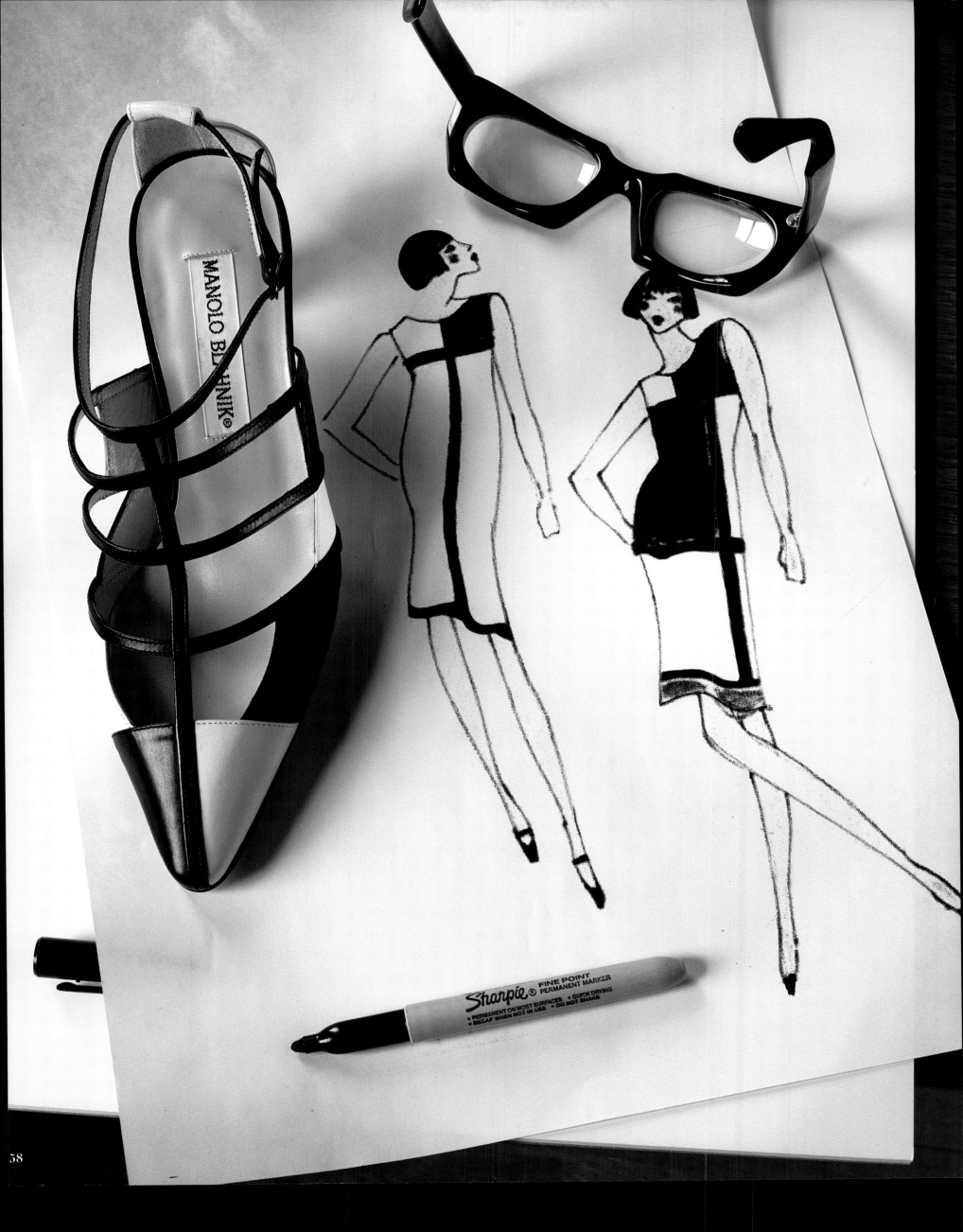

Francisco Zurbarán, Still Life, 1633. Oil on canvas © The Norton Simon Foundation.

ZUR

Norton Simon M

[53/54] Lacquer and wax! "Jungle Red"! The beauty parlour in "The Women". Excuse me, I have an appointment with Crystal. Isn't that Mrs Prowler over there? Those lipstick displays – and those names – were the epitome of glamour to me in the '50s. Paloma made her "Mon Rouge" by mixing her two favourite Revlon lipsticks together. [55/56] "Le Fanciulle del West"! On the dude ranch at the end of "The Women". L'amour, toujours l'amour! La publicité! [57/58] There's something Saint-Laurent about that boot … with a boot-tree from the Beaton sale. Yves is to me The God! I wanted to show your Mondrian as inspired by his Mondrians, in the presence of Yves, the handsome, glamorous, successful, in his lab coat. Now, these are the spectacles I insisted on having, in 1959. I feel an odd kinship in that. [59/60] Red gives one such a kick! Did you know that red and yellow are the first colours a child can see? You've told me that a hundred times! But this is very, very – close? Zurbaran means a lot to me. My visit to the Norton Simon/Jennifer Jones museum proved very useful. The wooden skull I carried all over Ecuador.... Chardin in the light of Vermeer. I thought more Fantin-Latour? I always had a foot in the eighteenth century. How did you train the bee? It takes a lot of patience. You could never do it! [61/62] Magritte chez Picasso! Paloma had a model of a 1920s couture salon that she thought might make a good prop. There were no pictures to go by, so I blindly picked a shoe that reminded me of Frank Lloyd Wright's Guggenheim Museum. The tall boot is inspired by the women of Borneo, who tattoo their limbs in wide horizontal stripes. How Genovese! But to me, it is an early nineteenth-century French soldier during the retreat from Moscow, as I saw it in "War and Peace" as an exam treat in 1956. That, and a scampi dinner.

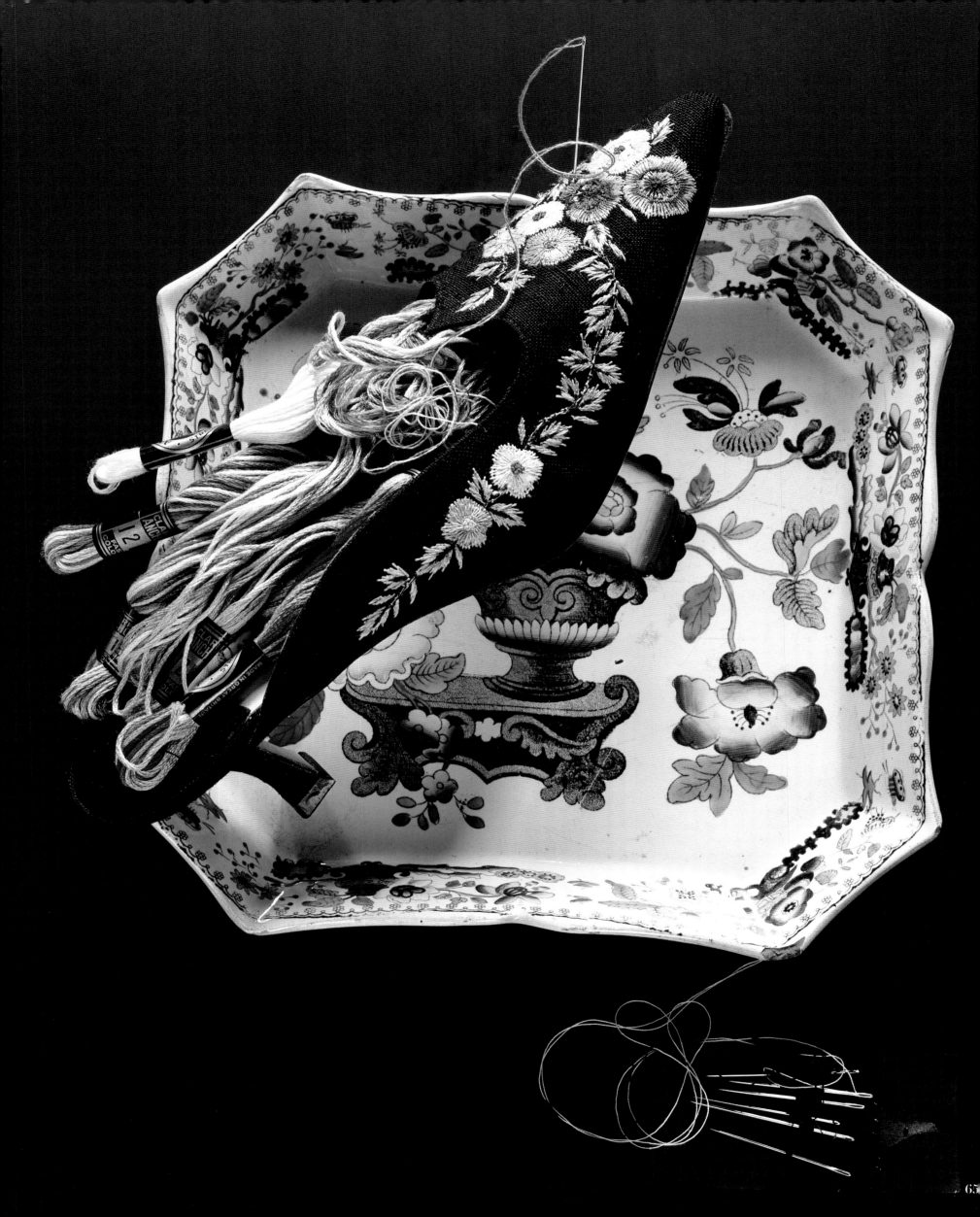

[63/64] A cocktail for Medusa. I have a thing about the half-open mouth of agony…. The young Maria Amalia Christina Franziska Xaveria Flora Walburga, Queen of Naples, and Maria Amalia to friends, suddenly felt faint-ish in the ballroom at Caserta, and was taken to a chair on the terrace, where the soft jasmine-scented evening air soon restored her. Meanwhile a strapping young lieutenant – how becoming a uniform can be! – with a very new, soft moustache, tenderly placed the shoe she had dropped on a chair, to save it for her return. [65/66] Europe versus Japan. The embroidery looks Swiss to me, but you should know, you went to school there. Fräulein Rottenmeier in a moment of solace. Heidi is dozing. The Japanese box of fans came from Peter's aunt. This is an image for Tina. Her spirit is somehow more present than those of others we have lost. It's about respect. Tina Chow forever! [67/68] Posing for Life Drawing class. Blahník and Linnaeus, the botanists. [69/70] It's the same dogwood tree in June and September. Birds love the fruit, but I haven't the nerve to taste one.… **A British "Vogue" cover with the embryonic model Maudie James in Pablo & Delia. [71/72] Cherries – these are Bigarreaux – are an old fixation** … of mine, too. In first grade, before we could write, we learned to count by drawing tiny pieces of fruit on graph-paper squares. I found it cheerful and reassuring. My favourites were cherries, two red dots connected by a green upside-down V for stalks. **The redcurrant shoe is from a painting of Paulina Bonaparte.** It came to me after my berries were over. If you look carefully, you'll see that these are fake ones I made from beads, with air bubbles in them that look like seeds, and green wire. It was such a buzz seeing the first cluster. I felt the taste of redcurrants on the palate!

[73/74] Is the eye of Gloria Swanson watching over me? Gloria was the story of Hollywood! Once you've read her autobiography, "Swanson on Swanson", you look at California with different eyes. Gloria may never have met Karen Blixen, although they would have liked each other, but I do know that Marilyn Monroe did. Many years later, I was photographing Blixen's house and needed some flowers. The curator showed me a charming book Blixen wrote on flower arranging, a passion of hers, so I could get in the spirit. She wanted flowers all the time, however modest, and would have been delighted to find this shoe. Her white lace living-room curtains were famously too long, but too good to cut, so they stretched out on the floor. The palm on the celery glass is symbolic ... of La Palma! [75/76] There's no story, I just went with the flow. These things happen! If it's any consolation to you, the frame had a picture of Doris Day – according to you, my mother – and Rock Hudson, which I took out to gain shadow play…. **My mother's shoemaker, Don Cristino, taught her to cobble, so she could have shoes when he went off to the war. These are the lasts she used.** Now your doorstops! [77] Mr MacBlahník's Highland holiday. **With a touch of Pérez Galdós's "Fortunata y Jacinta". The women of Madrid, in tartan taffeta – the height of Victorian sophistication.** There's a watercolour of a room at Balmoral, where, in the wishfulness of my decorating memory, the walls are Campbell of Breadalbane, the curtains are Dress Stewart, the Brussels carpet Graham, the runners MacDonald of the Isles, and the blond Biedermeier furniture is covered in MacLaine of Lochbuie with pillows in Macmillan, and footstools in Sinclair and bell-pulls in MacLeod. Plaid mad! The sheer luminous effect of check against check!

I bet it was a fear of clamouring clans that led Vicky and Bertie to forgo the room of their dreams and devise their own tartans. [78/79] **Strindberg's "Miss Julie" on ice, all things Swedish.** I thought this was where you'd get Romy Schneider in, from "Ludwig"? **In the snow, Anna Karenina! I'm convinced she didn't take her own life at all, but Vronsky pushed her.** I tried the boot on railroad tracks, but they were hidden under the snow. By the way, I saw my name written on the boot's kid lining!? **Yes, it's called "Boman".** I never knew that. **Of course you did! I made it for Anna Piaggi.** [80/81] The travel scene is what you might call "symbolisme recherché", or friendly incest. The suitcase from Peter's first trip to Europe had stickers on it from both Madrid and Prague. The sock is old stock from a time-warp menswear shop in Siracusa, on our way to meet you in Palermo, and the kerchief was my father's.

The jacket is yours, not mine. It's not very well made. What do you mean? It doesn't have a buttonhole on the lapel.... The antler picture is very Danish. Karen Blixen, again – or better still, Queen Gertrude at Elsinore! On clear days I could see the castle from my high school across the strait. [82/83] I did it years ago, all my windows with sculptor's mannequins.... I believe you! You know that I'm a toiletry case kind of person. One of the last, I should think. This one is mine, however. It has a bar of soap from Sicily and one of the kind my grandmother used in her house. The scent takes me back thousands of miles and forty-five years.

[84/85] The toy shoe in the toy shop! All this junk was in a box, unopened since my move to New York in 1978. What a thrill to see it again! Meanwhile, Veruschka, Countess von Lehndorff, is dressing for a photograph. She wrote me a sweet letter many years ago, saying she would like to buy a pair of boots, but the problem was that her feet were size eleven. I made them for her. In the beginning, before hair and makeup, the girls did their own faces, and the editor brought along hairpieces, which they attached like accessories. How simple, yet how effective! [86/87] Ah! Elegance in motion. The fencing scene from Visconti's "L'Innocente", with Marc Porel and Giancarlo Giannini. And the magical Mustang boot! The fan is turned off, but the feathery mane is still blowing. [88/89] Is it too soon to evoke the colourful bourgeois gaudiness of the 1980s? Belladonna – the dangerous drop of atropine – dilates your pupils and makes them darkly beautiful … but you'll need a guide dog. [90/91] Now, the nineteenth century in reverse, from end to beginning. The scent of auriculas has sweetness and mystery, like a perfume at a time when everyone wore black. Different blacks, depending on the cloth and dye: brown blacks, purple blacks, grey blacks. And everywhere shiny black cotton twill umbrellas, as in a Pissarro. Then, back to the Directoire, and the Princess Yusupov. Ornate uniforms and decorations, as in the Ingres portrait of Baron Joseph Vialètes de Mortarieu. For a foulard in the shoe, a pair of nylon gym shorts.… [92/93] The Christmas tree's chandelier prisms hang on the mosquito netting of the porch in July. Back to the future! Or a nuisance put to good use? A rude boatyard neighbour had smashed our windscreen with his protruding anchor. How unfortunate, but how ideal for a most favourite shoe!

[94/95] Mamie Eisenhower in Palm Beach … where a sprawling old Maurice Fatio house, empty and for sale, had this geranium print all over the patio furniture. The flower stall in Saint-Germain I used to pass on my way to work, before moving to London. Or along the side of the Madeleine, where they sold funny little posies of concentric bellis, with or without forget-me-nots. How French! [96/97] Trapped glamour! Sometimes we pay dearly for our enthusiasm. Do you remember the wedding dress of Fabiola Mora y Aragón as she became Queen of the Belgians? Balenciaga! Very severe! Silk satin duchesse with an edge of white ermine at the collar, which went in a straight line from shoulder to shoulder. I love columns, but this is not a column – it's only a display stand from Constance Spry. Am I perverse to find the crack in the urn delicious? [98/99] One day in the late '60s I spray-painted all my furniture in metallic pastels, including this gal who hung on the wall. She looks like Eija, the Finnish model. **Harold Acton and Palladio – transported to Sweden?** No, I found the chairs in a country junk shop there and transported them here.... [100/101] Who needs a fur coat when you can have steel wool? **The richest and the poorest!** Pretentiously, I like to think of the gold as a take on Italian Renaissance painting. The steel wool is lit by the moon – a very long exposure. [102/103] The first kitchen sink in a long succession.... **Zelda Fitzgerald knew it: when you kick your heels, they land all over the place.** [104/105] Guerlain's "Eau Impériale" and Yardley talcum powder. It's l'Entente Cordiale! I find the mood of that shoe so English, so Home Counties. **Gertrude and Alice knew how to live!** The "Alice B. Toklas Cook Book" is required reading around here. Butter is the main ingredient....

[106/107] My agenda is not specifically to put women back in front of the stove, but a glamorous woman cooking is not a contradiction in terms. My mother had red and white crocheted pot holders. **They do the crochet in Naples. It's what the hookers wear.… More kitchen sink drama: enamelled tinware made in Czechoslovakia!** [108/109] Now we're actually inside the wet sink, where a Spanish mackerel, a scale-less species, gets to feel what it would be like to have them. **Good evening! Tippi Hedren lost a shoe, running onto the pier in the water, where there was no escape from the stabbing beaks.** Finding the bird was pure Hitchcock in the present. A number in the Yellow Pages answered in a laboured woman's voice. "Taxidermy?" I asked. "Yes, he does that." Banging of stick on floor. I saw bedridden mother. Man's voice came on. "I'm looking for a crow or a blackbird," I said. "I have two," he replied. The next day

I drove up to the house, neatly suburban. All blinds were down. At the bottom of a window I saw bases of oxygen tanks – bedridden mother! I rang the bell. Banging of stick on floor. He came to the door, smiling. We made a deal. I borrowed the bird, photographed it and returned it. He said: "That guy with you, is he your friend?" I walked back to the car, knowing Norman Bates is alive and well and living on Long Island. [110/111] A taste of Agrigento! You know I don't drink alcohol, but I will take a drop of vodka and Campari if it's in freshly squeezed blood-orange juice. The apple picture I call "The Sodomy of Granny Smith". I call it "Husband Envy". [112/113] Our salad days! The colour of the suede is called "lechuga". I love that word. It has a beat! I think of the small leaves as purslane. Didn't know what it was until Claude Brouet told me my lawn is full of the pesky weed. She said it's so coveted as a salad green in

France that Taillevent adds a supplément to their prix fixe when it's available. But how did you know this? For me it was subconscious. Now I remember – I ate it all the time as a child! Doesn't that look like Marina Schiano on the bowl? [114/115] A pasticceria in Sorrento! But you know, I don't like the cookies very much. How can you not? They're all sugar! Of course I love meringues, but it's the pink ones, I don't like them. Too late. How about some sweetened condensed milk, which you drink with a straw, in a Swedish kitchen? A communion between our two cultures. La Lechera, May-Britt, the milkmaid! [116/117] How corny! The spaghetti strap – "Sedotta e Abbandonata" with a soupçon of garlic. Part of the reason I like Stephanie Seymour is because she reminds me of Stefania Sandrelli. They even have the same name! The raffia flat is inspired by what some Spanish peasants wear. It didn't

sell one pair! I'd wear it at once! Do you remember my set of china from Ponting's, the old department store on Kensington High Street? A full set for twelve, plus serving dishes, for £15. Things like that made it possible to live on next to nothing in those days. [118/119] **La Principessa sul Pisello! A portrait of the Hans Christian Andersen heroine, with apologies to Mr Penn.** My fascination with the titles of Rossini's ex-patriate operas, like "Mosè in Egitto", "L'Italiana in Algeri", "Il Turco in Italia", has made me fantasize that should I write an opera, I'd name it "L'Aragosta in Agosto", and centre it on a plot of food poisoning [much vomiting], to which the diva succumbs in the final act. This happy lobster became a tasty risotto at dinner time.

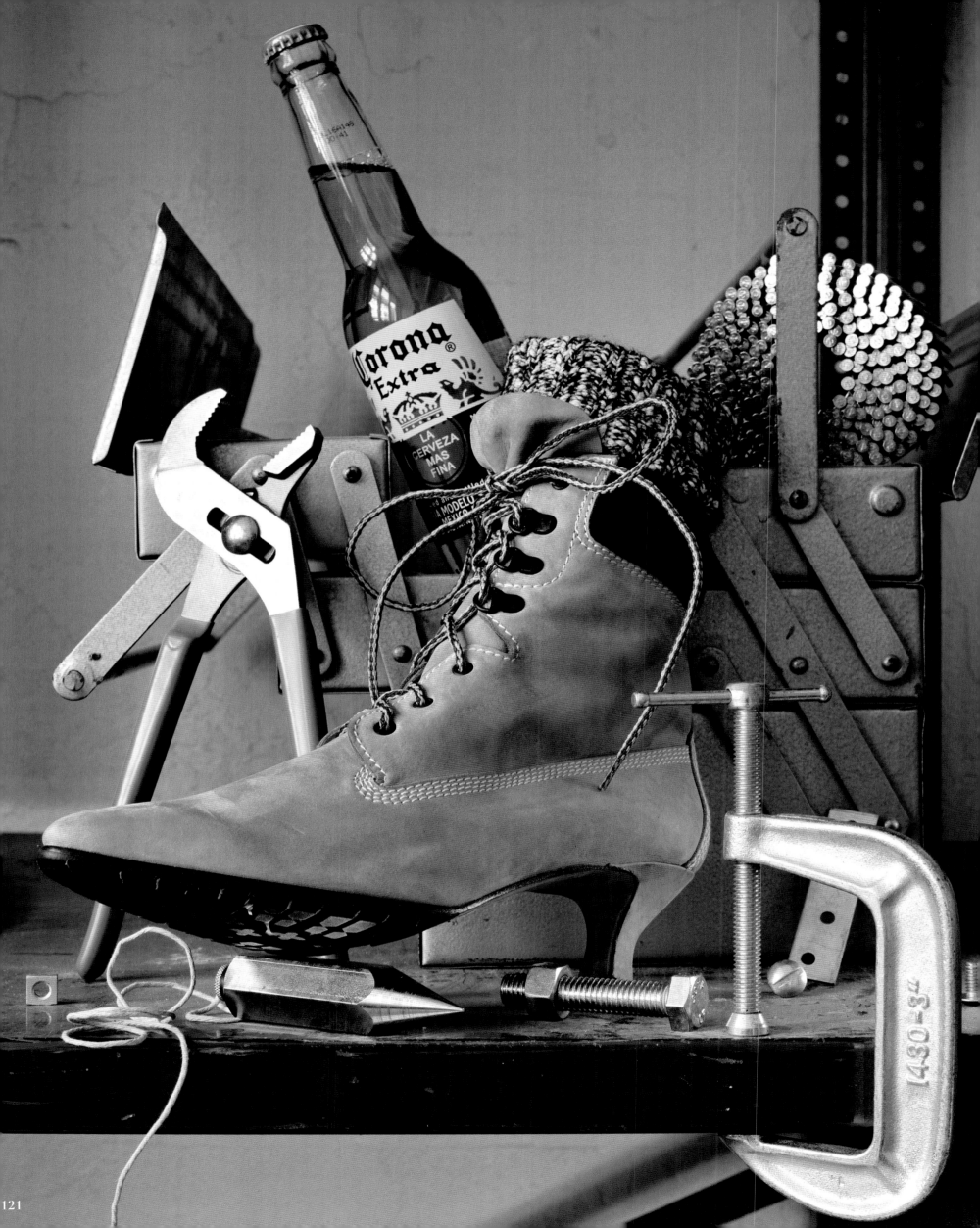

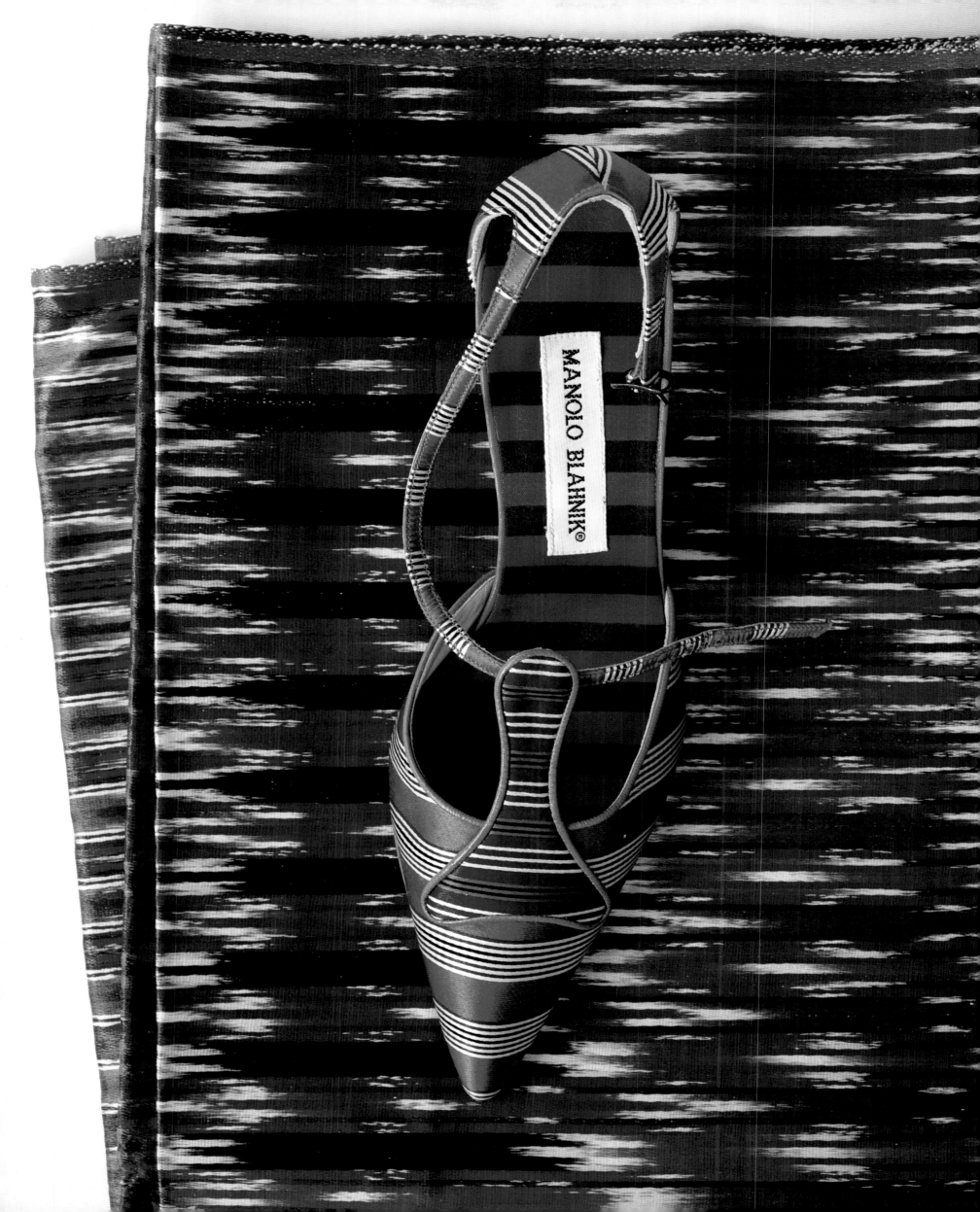

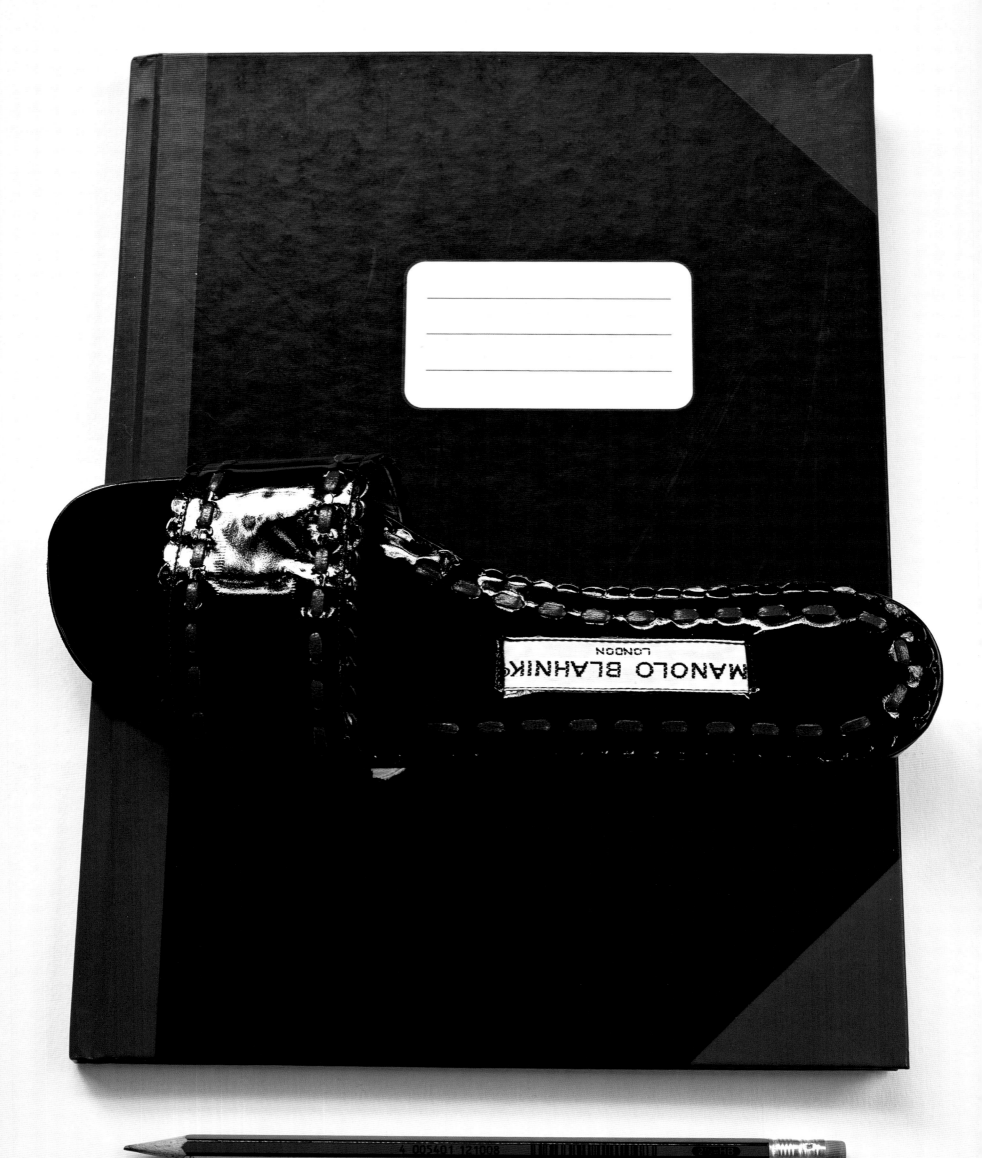

[120/121] Professional footwear. Please, no more kitchens! I'm also giving you butch…. That's the J-Lo boot. She knows her stuff. [122/123] Sometimes I read my cravings into your designs. An excuse to buy chocolates, photograph them and eat them…. Of animal bondage – or is he simply eating oats? [124] A Shoe Zoo! And also very gladiator … flesh for Poppaea! Please note: separate cages for carnivores and herbivores. [125/126] Death and decomposition equals renewal. These turtle shells and craniums are found in the garden, yet the turtle population is definitely on the increase. In the bayou of the pond, a hungry crocodile lurks. [127/128] Now, the travel section. An international cinematographic tour, from Bollywood to Cinecittà. The henna-painted hands of a young Hindu bride. "Cleopatra" on a low budget, as Marguerite [Littman] would say. [129/130] A Russian dacha and the souks of Damascus. That's where I bought the piece of fabric. The whole place smelled of pepper and rose-water. And there was a shop that sold doll's house furniture made of sugar. [131/132] **This Mondrian I love! On Broadway, doing the Boogie-Woogie! Maps are so evocative.** I once bought the "London A to Z" in Sweden and read it like a novel. By the time I got to London in 1965, I found my way everywhere.... Just looking at this map of Paris makes me nostalgic. [133/134] **Two Chinoiseries. Shanghai schoolgirl turns into Maggie Cheung, about to eat her take-out noodles, all alone in her cramped bed-sitter in Wong Kar Wai's "In the Mood for Love".** I, who never know where anything is, went straight for this shopping bag, saved from a trip to Hong Kong in 1973. In it was this receipt dated August 11. The power of the creative whim! If you put a gun to my head this very moment, I couldn't tell you where my glasses are....

WALTER ALBINI

MANOLO BLAHNIK

[135/136] My start in Milan. The clever and omnipresent Walter Albini. His beautiful flat in Venice. The Café Florian. Rooms with the heady perfume of gardenias. Grace Coddington wore Walter's little tweedy jersey suits and hats constantly, looking like Bette Davis in an early Warner Brothers movie. It's true, Walter's suits had the pretty proportions of Orry-Kelly! Although he didn't share an obsession with bows.... One day, walking past Peter's door, I heard this singing – I knew it when I was ten, but never what it was. Peter showed me this record he'd had since college in California. You know Chabela Vargas is alive – she's in an Almodóvar movie! This kind of coincidence is what makes life worth living for me.... But how did you know that the string I put around the heel was Mexican? Instinct! [137/138] The rose sandal – I made it for Givenchy, thinking of Paloma. All the mail you see is from her. Remember when we arrived at JFK in 1971, and Paloma met us in a Roman empress perm? **How we laughed at her! And she laughed, too!** She took us straight to see Andy and Fred, and Paul Morrissey who was editing with Jed, and Joe Dallessandro answered the door. **You nearly fainted!** They let us stay in the apartment Jane Forth and Donna Jordan had just moved out of, before Pat Hackett moved in. **New York was a different story with Andy there! [139/140] How precise you sometimes are.** Calder is very close to my heart, and obviously to yours, too. [141/142] The first time I saw you working on a shoe you were gluing the cherries on this one for Ossie Clark's show. **It was our fruity moment. I remember a cup you did at the Royal College of Art. It had cherries hanging over the rim.** Well, here they are – reunited! **I have to say, I like the tomato can a lot better than the shoe....**

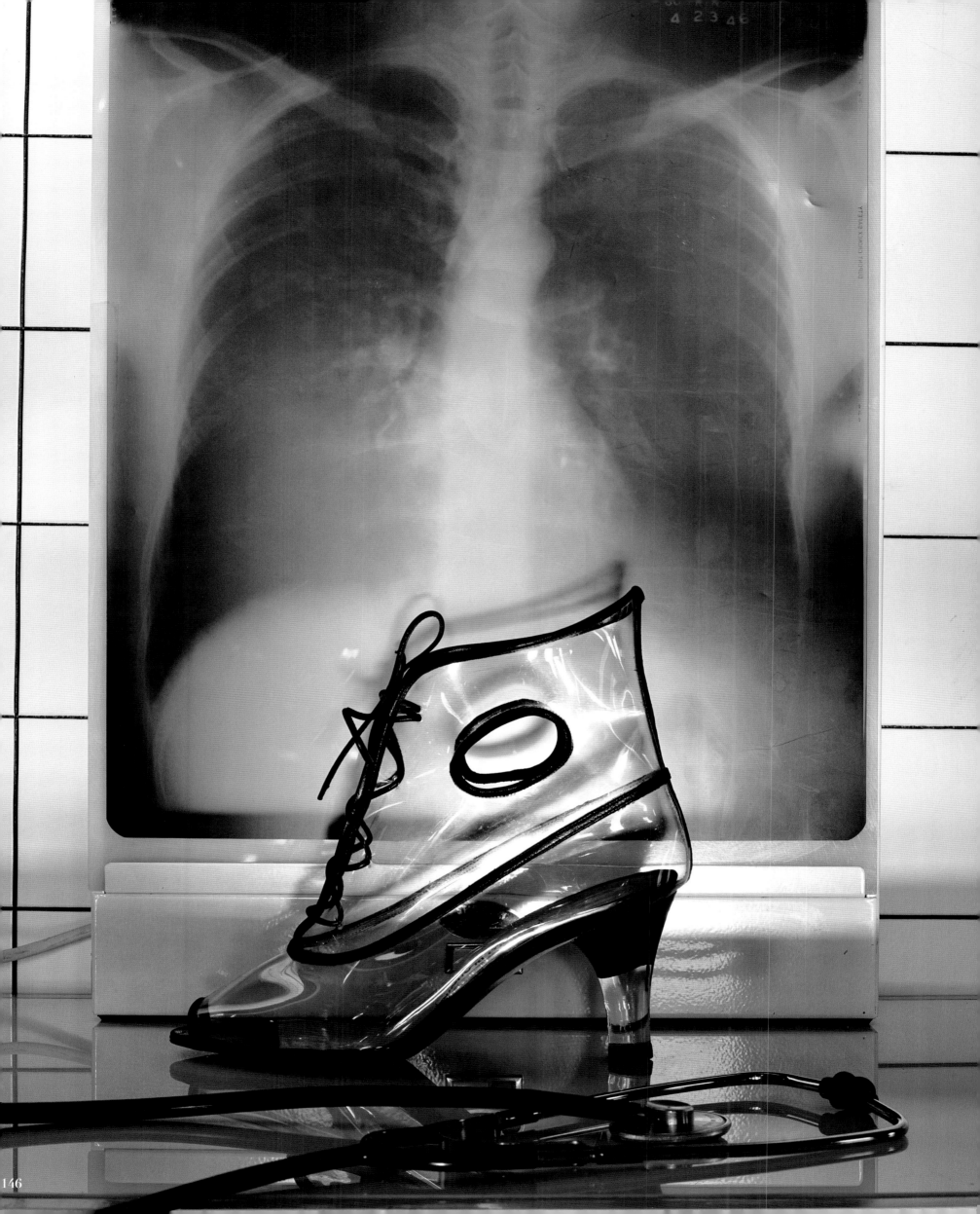

NYSTAN VAGINAL
Squibb (6D)

ALDACTONE-A
Searle (2B) (6B)

COTAZYM B
Organon (8B)

RAUWILOID
Riker (2B)

STELABID
S.K. & F (1C)

ASMAC
Wander (9C)

TANDERIL
Geigy (3B)

TRESCAZIDE
M. & B. (7D)

SENOKOT
Westminster (1D)

IVERSAL
F.B.A Pharm. (4B)

FERSAMAL
Glaxo (8E)

PREGAMAL
Glaxo (8E)

NYSTAN ORAL
Squibb (7A)

BECOVITE
Bencard (8F)

MANDELAMINE 0.5 G.
Warner (6A)

MANDELAMINE
0.25 G
Warner (6A)

GEVRAL
Lederle (8F)

NORM
Horlicks

FERROMYN B
Calmic (8E)

TRETAMINE
I.C.I. (8J)

NEO-FERRUM
Crookes (8E)

BEPLEX
Wyeth (8F)

PRIMAQUIN
I.C.I. (7G)

PHENSE
M. & B.

PYRIDIUM
Warner (6A)

PLESMET F.A.
Coates & Cooper
(8E)

DIBEXIN KAPSEALS
P. D. & Co. (8F)

DUROP
Riker

EPH
(9C)

ROMYN
ic (8E)

LEDERPLEX
Lederle (86)

PLASTULES with
LIVER EXTRACT
Wyeth (8E)

PLASTUL
Wyeth

N

PLESMET
Coates & Cooper
(8E)

EPHEDRINE and
NEMBUTAL
Abbot (8D)

IBEROL
Abbott (8E)

DIMOTAPP L.A.
Robins (8D)

FERROMYN B
Calmic (8E)

PERIHEMIN
Lederle (8F)

FERGON
Bayer (8E)

VI-MAGNA
Lederle (8F)

PLASTULES with
FOLIC ACID
Wyeth (8E)

PRENATAL
DRI-KAPS
Lederle (8F)

PREGFOL
Wyeth (8E)

DIBENYLINE
S. K. & F. (2B)

PREMARIN
0.625 mg.
I.C.I. (5A)

200 mg.
D)

UROPOL
Bristol (6A) (7A)

FERRAPLEX B
Bencard (8E)

BEPLETE
Wyeth (3D) (8F)

FERROGRAD C
Abbott (8E)

FERATE
(8E)

DYTAC
S. K. & F. (6B)

SKF SKF

SERENESIL
Abbott (3C)

PREGADAY
Glaxo (8E)

N 20 mg
r (3J)

CAPITUS
Berk (3E)

OR

DAYAMIN
Abbott (8F)

FOLVRON
Lederle (8E)

RIMACTANE
Ciba (7D)

FLEXAZONE
Berk (3B)

PARNATE
S. K. & F. (3J)

MANOLO BLAHNIK®

[143/144] Cause and effect. I love it! She slip [sic] and – boomba! – to the hospital. Helmut Newton was waiting by the elevator with his ring-flash. My mother's family had a banana plantation. Next door is now a power plant – it depresses me so much. [145/146] The cool glamour of nurses! The whole point of being ill! I was infatuated with one Sister Ruth. Then one day I saw her in her street clothes and the magic was just gone…. And here's my heart, proof that I put it in my work. [147/148] Pills and cigarettes! René Gruau! How influential his drawings were – just two, max three colours. Part of the era that had my mother give people a single long-stemmed red rose as the ultimate "elegant" gesture. Crashing! Jacqueline Susann's "Valley of The Dolls". [149/150] A sacristy composition. Stuck in my mind is a scene from a movie where young priests run up and down the steps of a Baroque church.

A breathless Anita Ekberg in the dark of the confessional, repenting for taking that dip in "La Dolce Vita" … while outside, in the wicked street, Helmut is photographing the tuxedoed Vibeke propositioning the naked Eija. [151/152] Madame Rochas and the Marquesa de Alba! Those dishes are yard-sale 1960s Limoges for Marcel Rochas. And that bed is the one you sleep in when you visit. The effect is very Spanish, no? [153/154] Margot Fonteyn changing into a very short YSL feather dress for supper with Rudy. Did you know she was part swan? Stuff your shoes with acid-free tissue paper and they'll keep their shape! [155/156] Your Gothic stalactites on Karel Plicka's book of Prague. Are you crazy? This is Czech! How did you know? As a boy, my father sang in the choir at the Chapel of St Wenceslas! A little Lutheran gloom, to temper the merriment. Ingrid Thulin in Bergman's "Nattvardsgästerna".

[157/158] For better or worse, not being a writer, I'm free from writer's block…. Opposite, a late Lady Amherst pheasant in an attempt at Mannerism. Well, I'm sorry – not very convincing. To me it all looks Dickensian. [159/160] I understand exotic chickens are all the rage – how Chatsworth! As you see, they will lay just about anywhere. The widow shoe – it depressed everybody! Mrs Onassis sat next to me at Mrs Vreeland's memorial service. She was like nobody else; through all the dramas of her life, a uniquely calm presence. [161/162] You were always mimicking Dalida, the beehive-haired Egyptian starlet on French television, singing this song. That's our family piano, not tuned for thirty years. Horsehair and astrakhan. Order in the court! But, I have to say, I don't like lawyers. [163/164] At the bodega. The guitar is the Spanish instrument, even in toy form. How fabulous! They're from the Canary Islands!

I hate to disappoint, but they're actually from a street market outside Managua. Think of them as a connection with Bianca's country! The queens of Las Folclóricas! Juanita Reina! Lola Flores! Estrellita Castro! Eastman Color at the movie houses! I was six or seven, so this is very special for me. The shoes of the street singers, with fringed ribbons circling their legs. The songs of Antonio Molina. The violent gyrations of Carmen Amaya. You don't know any of this? Eric, you're not very cultured! [165/166] Mmm! Incense and coral, the scent and colour of my youth. Of mine, iodine, pine resin and shells. Miraculously, the beach looks the same all year. Different shells wash up with different currents, and the light changes all the time, but basically it's reliable. [167/168] New England! Boston baked beans! L.L. Bean! High-heel gardening and picnic by the swimming hole.